W9-CLM-686

ANIMAL SOS!

SAVE THE

GIANT PANDA

WINDMILL BOOKS
New York

Published in 2014 by Windmill Books, An Imprint of Rosen Publishing
29 East 21st Street, New York, NY 10010

Produced for Windmill by Calcium Creative Ltd
Editors for Calcium Creative Ltd: Sarah Eason and Rachel Blount
US Editor: Joshua Shadowens
Designer: Emma DeBanks

Photo Credits: Cover: Shutterstock: Fstockfoto.
Inside: Dreamstime: Carmentianya 22, 28, Donyanedomam 13, Engraver 11,
Hanbaoluan 12, Hungchungchih 29, Hupeng 21, Jmphoto 25, Kbuffo7 17,
Leesniderphotoimages 16, Lukyslukys 10, Maxfx 23, Raywoo 18,
Silverjohn 1, 26, Zhaoyineptune 6, 15; Shutterstock: Wen Billy 14, Hung
Chung Chih 19, 20, 24, Davidelliottphotos 8, Df028 27, Leungchopan 4,
Silver-John 9, Worldgraphics 5, Pan Xunbin 7.

Library of Congress Cataloging-in-Publication Data

Royston, Angela, 1945–
Save the giant panda / by Angela Royston.
pages cm. — (Animal SOS!)
Includes index.
ISBN 978-1-4777-6042-0 (library) — ISBN 978-1-4777-6035-2 (pbk.) —
ISBN 978-1-4777-6047-5 (6-pack)
1. Giant panda—Conservation—Juvenile literature. 2. Endangered
species—China—Juvenile literature. I. Title.
QL737.C214R69 2014
599.789—dc23
2013025830

Manufactured in the United States of America

CPSIA Compliance Information: Batch #BW14WM: For Further Information contact Windmill Books, New York, New York at 1-866-478-0556

Contents

Pandas in Danger

Giant pandas are large, gentle bears. Their black eye patches and ears make them one of the easiest animals to recognize. Almost everyone loves pandas, but there may soon be none left.

Why Are Pandas Threatened?

People have been trying to save pandas for more than 50 years, so why are they still in danger of becoming **extinct**? The main reason is that people are taking over the natural countryside where the pandas live. Another reason is that giant pandas do not easily produce cubs.

The shape of a panda's head and body is similar to other bears. However, no other bears have the same black and white markings.

Getting to Know the Panda

Scientists study how pandas live and what they need to survive. Saving pandas costs a lot of money. This book will tell you what you can do to help save these amazing animals.

Young pandas like to play, but adult pandas spend almost all their time either eating or sleeping.

Rescue the PANDA!

You can help by raising money to send to **charities** that work to protect pandas. Find out all you can about the pandas, and try to persuade your friends and family to help raise money, too.

Where Pandas Live

Pandas live in forests in western China. Most bears eat meat, but pandas are unusual because they eat the **bamboo** that grows beneath the forest trees. Most of the bamboo forests that still remain in China are in the mountains.

Mountain Homes

For thousands of years, many pandas lived in Burma, Vietnam, and right across southern and eastern China. Now, scientists estimate that only around 1,600 adult pandas still live in the wild, mostly in the Qinling and Minshan mountains, between China and Tibet.

The hillsides and rugged tops of the Qinling mountains are covered with forests of trees and bamboo.

Bamboo Diet

A panda's diet is made up almost entirely of bamboo. The pandas' favorite food is the young shoots, leaves, and stems of arrow bamboo and umbrella bamboo. Pandas have a special wrist bone that they use like a thumb to grasp the bamboo.

The bamboo plant grows incredibly quickly. It can grow up to 98 feet (30 m) tall, depending on the type of bamboo.

ANIMAL SOS!

Umbrella bamboo grows only on land between 1,650 feet (500 m) through 10,000 feet (3,100 m) high. This limits the areas where pandas can easily survive. Arrow bamboo grows lower down the mountainside.

Can Pandas Defend Themselves?

Pandas are shy, peaceful animals. They live on their own for most of the time and avoid other animals. However, other animals also live in bamboo forests. If necessary, pandas can defend themselves against other animals.

Panda Weapons

A panda's strongest weapon is the weight of its body. If a panda rolled on top of you, you would be crushed. Like other bears, pandas have strong jaws and sharp teeth. Although pandas are **vegetarian**, their teeth can easily rip through flesh.

A panda may look cute, but do not be deceived. Its teeth can deliver a dangerous bite.

Time to Go!

If an animal annoys a panda, it will not attack immediately. Instead, it lowers its head and stares! This warns the other animal to go away. Pandas themselves can escape danger by swimming across rivers or climbing trees. Panda cubs are especially great tree climbers.

Cubs love to climb trees and use their skill to scramble to safety when they are threatened by danger on the ground.

Rescue the PANDA!

Only a few zoos in the United States have pandas. If one of these zoos is near you, try to visit it and then tell your classmates about the pandas you have seen.

The Pandas' Enemies

Only a few animals dare to attack these big bears. Predators include jackals, leopards, and yellow-throated martens. Snow leopards, in particular, attack panda cubs. However, the pandas' greatest enemies are people.

Poaching Pandas

In the past, local people used to hunt giant pandas because they could sell their fur for large sums of money. Since the 1990s, however, Chinese people have learned how rare pandas are, and now most people protect them. Anyone who does kill a panda is severely punished by law.

Yellow-throated martens and pandas drink water from the same mountain streams. The martens are known to attack panda cubs.

Destroying the Forests

Today, people are harming pandas by taking over the wild bamboo forests in which they live. Just 100 years ago, pandas lived all along the mountains between China and Tibet. Today, they have just a few small patches of forest in which to live.

Snow leopards live in the same high mountains as the pandas. They prowl through the forests, hunting for panda cubs and other prey.

ANIMaL SOS!

Some patches of forest are too small for more than one or two pandas to live in. Two adult pandas need at least 12 square miles (3,108 ha) of forest to themselves to find enough bamboo to survive.

Losing Ground

Pandas are picky about their food, so they cannot live just anywhere. At one time, the bamboo they feed on grew widely in parts of China, but today the forests are disappearing.

People Need Land, Too

As the population in China increases, local people need more land for farms and homes. Most of the forests on the lower slopes of the mountains have already been cleared, and farmers are moving onto higher slopes. There is now little land left for pandas below 4,600 feet (1,400 m).

Today, villages are being built higher up the mountains than ever before. This means that more of the pandas' forests are being cleared for crops and houses.

Isolated Patches

Only 20 patches of forest where pandas still survive in the wild remain. Many of the patches are too far apart for pandas to travel from one to the other. Other patches are narrow strips of land no more than 0.75 miles (1.2 km) wide.

ANIMAL SOS!

The Qinling mountains are home to many different types of animals. These include golden monkeys, clouded leopards, and golden eagles, all of which are also **endangered species**. Saving the pandas will help to save these animals, too.

The areas in which pandas live are under threat and these wonderful bears are struggling to survive in small patches of land.

Dams, Mines, and Roads

Many pandas live in the Qinling mountains. This is an important area where mining takes place and electricity is **generated**. The people who carry out these activities compete with the pandas for any available space.

Electricity and Mining

People need electricity. In China, some electricity is generated by building **dams** in the Qinling mountains, to trap water. The Qinling mountains also contain valuable metals, such as gold, silver, lead, and zinc, which companies are keen to mine.

When a dam is built, the land behind the dam is flooded, destroying all the forest in the valley. This dam is being built in Tibet, on the border of panda territory.

Taking Up Space

Dams, mines, and other industrial projects take up a huge amount of space. This is space that cannot be preserved for wildlife. Roads are built through the mountains to link the mines to the cities. The roads open up the forests to people, and break up the pandas' **habitat** into smaller and smaller patches.

Roads built through the mountains break up the pandas' territory, and bring more people into the panda's area.

Rescue the PANDA!

Join a charity, such as Panda International or the World Wildlife Fund (WWF), which work to save pandas. Look up the charities on the Internet and find out how they spend the money they receive to preserve land for the pandas.

Losing Bamboo

Even the forest that remain are not safe for pandas. People cut down the trees and sell the wood. Bamboo also dies back naturally around every 30 years.

Useful Plant

Bamboo is a type of grass and one of the fastest growing plants. Its hollow, woody stalks are used to make tables, chairs, chests, and other furniture. It is even used to make the walls of houses.

Green stems of newly cut bamboo are tied together in bundles at factories. This factory is in Sichuan Province, China, where many pandas live.

Big Appetite

Each adult panda eats around 22 pounds (10 kg), or more, of bamboo every day. Pandas spend at least 12 hours a day picking and eating the juiciest bamboo shoots. If the bamboo runs out, the pandas move on, if they can.

ANIMAL SOS!

Bamboo grows for years before it produces any flowers. As soon as it has flowered, it dies back. In the past, it did not matter if a large area of bamboo suddenly disappeared. The pandas simply moved on. Now, if they have nowhere to go, they starve.

Pandas love to sit around eating young shoots of juicy bamboo!

Helping Pandas

Charities help pandas in two main ways. They raise money by making people aware of the problems facing pandas. Then, they use the money to help protect the pandas.

Nature Reserves

The best way to protect wild pandas is to protect the land where they live. These protected areas are called **nature reserves** and around half of all wild pandas live in reserves. Charities work with the Chinese government to help **environmentalists** set up and run the reserves.

Many tourists visit nature reserves, such as Huanglong Nature Reserve, in Sichuan, to enjoy the amazing scenery, as well as look for pandas.

Dealing with Tourism

Some nature reserves raise extra money by encouraging tourists to visit the reserves. The tourists learn about the work of the reserves, and local people make money from tourists. Tourism has to be carefully controlled, however, because too many visitors disturb the pandas.

Pandas can hide among the leaves in a thick forest, and keep a look out at the same time.

Rescue the PANDA!

Organizing a panda picnic is a fun way of making your friends aware of pandas. Invite your friends to dress up as pandas, and play panda-themed games. If possible, choose a picnic place where you can climb trees safely.

Nature Reserves

Making an area into a nature reserve is not enough to save the pandas that live there. The reserve must be well run and all the pandas must be protected from poachers.

Wolong Nature Reserve

The first nature reserve for pandas was set up in 1963 at Wolong, near Chengdu. It is the largest reserve and the most popular reserve for tourists. In 1981, a research center was set up in the reserve. The center helps **captive** pandas to produce cubs.

In Chengdu, the easiest place to see pandas is in the Research Base.

Protecting Pandas

Although killing pandas is illegal, poachers set traps to catch musk deer, black bears, and other animals. Sometimes, a panda is accidentally caught in a trap, and is hurt or killed. Guards patrol the reserve to prevent poaching and to look for sick or injured pandas.

Pandas are safer in a nature reserve than in the wild, but they are not completely safe from poachers and natural disasters.

ANIMAL SOS!

In 2008, a terrible earthquake occurred close to Wolong Nature Reserve. More than 70,000 people died, including five of the reserve's guards. Two pandas at the research center were killed, but no one knows how many wild pandas also died.

Panda Cubs

The number of pandas in the wild will only increase if wild pandas have lots of babies. Pandas **reproduce** slowly, and they need to be part of a large group to meet a **mate**.

Linking Groups

How can **conservationists** link up groups of pandas to help them mate? The answer is to make a bamboo corridor between the pandas. This not only helps the pandas to produce cubs, but it also gives them somewhere to go when an area of bamboo dies back.

Panda cubs love to climb among trees. The cubs grow fast. By the time they are one year old, cubs weigh between 70 and 80 pounds (32–36 kg).

Planting a Corridor

For 23 years, a busy road separated two reserves in the Qinling mountains. When a road tunnel was built through the mountain, the old road was abandoned. Volunteers then planted bamboo along 8 miles (13 km) of the road to link the two groups of pandas.

Rescue the PANDA!

Ask your teacher if your class can raise money for pandas after school. You could organize a bake sale and sell homemade cupcakes and cookies. If you cannot do this at school, ask your parents if you can do it at home.

Panda mothers care for their cubs for around two years. The cubs are very small when they are born, weighing just 6 ounces (170 g).

Pandas On Loan

The Chinese government lends pandas to zoos in other countries. Pandas are big news, particularly if they produce a cub. After several years of being away from their original zoo, the pandas return to China.

Good News for Zoos

Giant pandas are probably the biggest attraction a zoo can have. It costs the zoo around $1.5 million a year to **lease** the pandas and to care for them. However, so many people pay to see the pandas that the zoo can easily make this money back.

Giant panda cubs are always big news. A year after twin panda cubs were born at Chengdu, in 2012, the reserve invited television crews and news photographers to film them on their first birthday.

More Money for Pandas

The pandas that are lent to zoos are captive pandas from Chinese zoos. Lending pandas brings in money for the Chinese government, up to $1 million a year for each panda. China uses this money to pay for research into pandas, and to protect giant pandas in the wild.

ANIMAL SOS!

You might think that even if pandas die out in the wild, they will always exist in zoos. This is not necessarily so, however, because it is hard to get captive pandas to **breed**.

A giant panda, on loan from China, makes itself at home in the National Zoo in Washington, D.C.

Pandas in Zoos

Zoos do not lease pandas only to make money for the zoo. Keeping a pair of pandas in the zoo gives scientists the opportunity to study the bears up close for several years.

Captive Pandas

Around 300 giant pandas are held in zoos, mostly in China. In 2013, four zoos in the United States had pandas, Atlanta, San Diego, Memphis, and the National Zoo, in Washington, D.C. In March 2013, two pandas arrived in a special airplane at Toronto, in Canada. Canada's prime minister even met the pandas at the airport!

A panda cub takes a nap in a tree, in Chengdu zoo, in China. It may look unsafe, but it is securely wedged between the branches.

26

Waiting for Cubs

A female panda gives birth to just one or two cubs at one time. She is able to become pregnant just once a year, and then only during a few hours. Scientists desperately want to help pandas produce more cubs in captivity.

Rescue the PANDA!

If you cannot visit a zoo to see pandas, visit the zoos' websites instead. Click on the live **camcorders** to see what the pandas are doing at that moment. Use the cameras to visit the pandas every day!

Pandas in zoos have more time to play than pandas in the wild. They particularly enjoy playing with toys and climbing on frames.

27

Will Wild Pandas Survive?

It is difficult to save pandas. Panda protection also costs a lot of money, far more than for most other endangered animals. Thankfully, scientists are now making progress in protecting pandas.

What Is the Aim?

For pandas to survive, they need more bamboo forest in which to live, and to give birth to many more cubs. Conservationists are replanting land with bamboo and linking existing patches of forest. Zoos are also getting better at helping pandas to breed in captivity.

Like all young animals, panda cubs like to play. When they are young, they play with their mother, but older cubs play with each other.

One Cub, or Two?

Although pandas often give birth to twins, the mother will care only for one of the cubs. To encourage a panda to care for both of her cubs, researchers keep one newborn cub in an **incubator**. Then they swap the cubs repeatedly, without the mother realizing. Both of the panda cubs survive.

Zookeepers keep a careful watch on cubs born in captivity. This two-month-old cub is being checked by a member of the zoo's staff.

ANIMAL SOS!

At the moment, cubs born in captivity do not survive in the wild. The aim for scientists is to train captive pandas and cubs to slowly become used to living in the wild.

Glossary

bamboo (bam-BOO) A tall grass with a woody stem.

breed (BREED) To come together to produce cubs.

camcorders (KAM-kor-durz) Video cameras that record sound and movement.

captive (KAP-tiv) When an animal lives in a zoo, or an aquarium, instead of living in the wild.

charities (CHER-uh-teez) Organizations that collect money from people and spend it to help those in need.

conservationists (kon-sur-VAY-shun-ists) People who act to protect the environment.

dams (DAMZ) Barriers across rivers that trap water behind them.

endangered species (in-DAYN-jurd SPEE-sheez) A type of living thing, such as the giant panda, that is in danger of becoming extinct.

environmentalists (in-vy-run-MEN-tuh-lusts) People who act to protect the environment.

extinct (ik-STINGKT) No longer existing.

generated (JEH-nuh-rayt-ed) Produced.

habitat (HA-buh-tat) A particular type of environment, such as forests or deserts.

incubator (ING-kyuh-bay-ter) A special box that helps to keep a newborn animal alive.

lease (LEES) To pay a sum of money, to borrow something.

mate (MAYT) A member of the opposite sex with which an animal can breed.

nature reserves (NAY-chur rih-ZURVZ) Areas of land where plants and animals can live safely.

poachers (POH-churz) People who kill wild animals illegally, usually for food or body parts.

reproduce (ree-pruh-DOOS) To produce young.

vegetarian (veh-juh-TER-ee-un) A person, or animal, that does not eat meat.

Further Reading

Keller, Susanna. *Meet the Panda*. At the Zoo. New York: PowerKids Press, 2010.

Portman, Michael. *Pandas in Danger*. Animals at Risk. New York: Gareth Stevens Learning Library, 2011.

Schreiber, Anne. *Pandas*. National Geographic for Kids. Washington, D.C.: National Geographic Children's Books, 2010.

Websites

For web resources related to the subject of this book, go to: www.windmillbooks.com/weblinks and select this book's title.

Index